Love,

Tiana

Tiana Harewood

Dear You,

I love you. I realize that many of us don't hear it as often as we should, but I need you to know that you are loved. Love is not linear. It doesn't follow a specific outline. I think it gets overwhelming when we try to place it within a specific framework for the sake of understanding. Just as we cannot explain the extent of He who is Love, we cannot deduce the experience of love to an arrangement of beautiful words.

This collection explores love on a spectrum from broken to healed. It highlights the love of God, the love for others, and the love of self. Some of the pieces include fragments of my personal love journey. I hope that my transparency adds language to pieces of your love.

Sis/Bro, I dedicate this work to you. You who strive to love and desire to be loved. It gets hard; to love God, love people, and receive love from both, but you're treasured, capable, and worthy.

Love,
Tiana

.

Table of Contents

Broken   **6**

Healing   **41**

Healed   84

freelance
love
patient with love
the one
formed
photo
regular love

broken.

Love, Tiana

Dear You,

*Healing doesn't mean everything
will feel better all the time.
Sometimes you will feel like the
hurt, pain, and pressure you're
recovering from is pulling you back.
I want you to know that it is an
illusion. Healing requires exposure,
and exposure provokes pain. This
pain is a symptom of the
disinfectant of hope making room.
Although it feels familiar, it's
birthing something new in you.*

*Love,
Tiana*

losing

I thought I knew what I wanted
What I was to be
What I was to become,
But I didn't.

I thought I had released
expectations and old versions of
hurt, but I still feel it.

The disappointment, the festered
hurt, the torn expectation, the
broken heart.. it's still here.

It still rattles when I speak through
disagreements. It shakes during
the silent contemplation of words
that describe my hurt and feelings.

I'm not supposed to be feeling.
I'm supposed to be healing.

Love, Tiana

The feelings should be on pause
because there's cruelty in adding
vinegar to wounds and that's what
this feels like.

What is this for?
Why?
Why add sting to my pain?

I've been burned, bombed, cut,
scraped, pushed, punched,
bruised, and scarred. Now, I'm
stung left to crumble under the
waves of pain.

Is this it?

Healing to feel.
Feeling to heal.
That's enough!
I'm done.

I no longer subscribe to this
channel of static playing late at
night as I try to find the rest of the
rest I've been longing for.

9

The safety to be and stretch and
cry and feel and heal and fail and
fall and win... when will I win?
That's what this is about.

I feel like I'm losing a game I
should've never played.

Well created.
Without instructions.
I'm failing.
No rules.
No partner.
No phone a friend.
Just me.
Losing.

Dear You,

Hoping for something to happen doesn't guarantee that it will happen when, how, where, or with whom you want it to. However, you must keep hope alive. Consider that disappointment is your hope's proof of life so that you're not shattered when it comes.

Love,
Tiana

unbreak my heart

Unbreak my heart
Or what's left of it

I have the glue and time
But not the mind

I'm damaged

Irreparably shattered
By the tatters of broken covenant

I'm hopeless

Undeniably down
And crowned with inconceivable
doubt

Tomorrow lied

He promised that my tears had
purpose
But the unnamed purpose left me
nervous

Unsure if I mistook his intention,
Or misunderstood his attention.
I have questions.

Why'd you lie?
Or maybe you didn't.

Maybe my affections were
misplaced

Maybe I held an aimless hope
And shot into a void
You avoided.

I'm sorry.
It's just that you,
I mean Tomorrow left me

Overwhelmed,
Unheard,
Still broken,
And lifeless

'Cause when I lived - I hoped
And when I hoped - I lost
When I lost - I begged
When I begged - it cost

So here lies my proof of life
She ran a good race
And fought a good fight

Long live this heart of mine
Shaped by the deferred hope
Tomorrow enshrined.

Dear You,

Betrayal will happen. When betrayal happens, you have a choice; Either allow the moment to become a season or use the moment as data to move forward in love with intention. Choose ye this day.

Love,
Tiana

betrayal

I trusted you.
I thought you were safe.
I let you hold my hand and wipe
my tears
I let you into my space to feel my
fears

Do you feel that?

The shadows of safety you so
easily lent me only to pull back the
covering exposing the dark pieces
of me.

I tried for you.
I tried for me.
I needed you to see the real me
but
I don't know maybe
I should've stuck to the scripted
me
The clothed in my right mind me

Instead of thinking you had the
capacity to capture the weight of
me like a piece of photography
pausing to note the frame and
light frozen in time.

But here I am left in dim lighting
Fighting to keep what honor I have
left.

Why do I have to fight for my light
when what you did wasn't right?

It wasn't my fault you weren't
worthy and your dishonor didn't
serve me.

I just wanted you to love me.
Love me for me
but me was too much for you
and I'm too much for fools.

You fool!

I trusted you
and only fools allow themselves to
be wrapped up in a spool of
betrayal marrying every
relationship that failed to the tales
of a fool.

Fool, allow me to school you on
what you couldn't do.

Dear You,

If you choose to date after heartbreak, don't. Take time to sit with yourself, ask yourself hard questions and answer soberly. Rushing into the next relationship will only reveal that you are careless with yourself and others. Some will hurt the next person, while others will hurt themselves. Let's end the cycle of hurt people.

Love,
Tiana

touché

I've played a lot games
And won a lot of trophies
Stole a lot of hearts
Was everything but holy

I know that sounds bad
But I'm not completely soul-less
I once was a lover
Until I turned hopeless

Chained to yesterday's heartbreak
I had a wounded soul
Eager to prove myself worthy
To be kept, to be whole

But I didn't have a manual
How was I to know the truth
That my worth could be the same
And my heart be torn in two

So I turned off my feelings
And Turned on my pride
Then Turned up my ego

And turned down my light

I made a plan for the next guy
To make him pay
For everything I lost
And everything I gave

You would think I was baller
The way I crossed over and laid up
Number one draft pick
My game was up and stuck

Then I met a player
Who knew the game a little better
He played me like the playoffs
Set a new shooting record

I knew his game was fierce
But I thought I had a chance
To make him see the wounded me
So he could change my plan

His game matched mine
Which made me want more
But he was too much to handle
A beast on the court

21

Love, Tiana

See his pain was much deeper
Which made his game tight
Nobody could really see him
Cause he'd turned down his light

Two wounded souls
Playing for a win
Forfeiting our healing
For an unexpected end

I faked to the left
He caught me on the right
I fell to the ground
Then got up ready to fight

Cause why can't he see
We're the perfect match
We're hurt the same way
I'm the perfect catch

He drove the ball to the goal
To make the winning shot
In it went and then he smiled
My plan was all for naught

Love, Tiana

He came to me and said good
game
Stuck out his hand to shake
I said you're right and walked away
And named that game touché.

Dear You,

I wasn't born saved. There were many times where God kept me when I didn't care to be kept. I grabbed every bit of control I thought I had and strayed away from him. It was his mercy by way of His love that protected me. Sis/Bro, His love is so vast that even when you're stupid, His love covers you.

Love,
Tiana

fistful of offense

One two check boom
There goes the room that was
spinning
And the man that was grinning
Thinking he would win the finish

Instead, Mother Nature came to
town and slowed me down and
stole his crown of glory allowing
God to shift the story.

I spent the night in rest, laid out
like a damsel in distress instead of
undressing to impress a man left
unkept

He stayed with me, took care of
me, made sure I was kept and
never overstepped the invisible
bounds laid around me.

He knew I wasn't my own and I
had strayed away from home. I
asked for my freedom and my
Father let me meet him 'cause
despite the grin and sin he was in
he knew I didn't fit in.

15 by looks.
17 by age.
19 by lie.
It wasn't a surprise when the lies
multiplied. He was a "friend" to
mom, a familiar face to see.
But a stranger by default, chosen
to rescue me.

It could've been worse.
Found in the dirt, by the sea.
Bloodied skirt on the scene for
everyone to see what could've
been.

Sad story of a girl with potential
by a perp without credentials.

What could've been, wasn't. What
should've been, doesn't
amount to the grace that was
placed on my life before I came to
this place in life.

My plan eroded when His path
unfolded and took me from hoe to
holy. From broken to boldly
leaving a night where I was guilty
and filthy adding to the existing
empty but He filled me.

It was giving dumb and numb to
the taste of grace. Wasting good
sense on a pretense that
intentions were well meant. Yolo
was spent in a body that lent a
fistful of offense

Dear You,

Lust is deceptive. It will whisper sweet nothings to lead you to sweet nothings. You will lose more than you think you're gaining when you give into its provocations. Sis/Bro, you're too wealthy, too smart, and too discerning to be deceived because you lack self-control. Just because you crave it does not mean you need it.

Love,
Tiana

lust liar

Lust, You lied to me
You dirty nasty bleep
Every time I asked of you
You obliged my every need

Even when I was too full to ask
You told me to make room
Then brought to me my favorite
flask
And reveled in my doom

What I had just wasn't enough
You told me I needed more
To fill my voids with pointless stuff
So you continued to pour

Men were things
I put high on my shelf
Collector's items
Kept all to myself

Love, Tiana

They served me well
Mirroring my pride inside

Until I snatched back the masks
To find lust in disguise

You stole from me
So, a lying thief is what you are
Stealing time and prime
And raising the goal bar

You said I needed more
to sway resentment
to keep my value
to find contentment

But I didn't need more
I needed self-control
To tell myself to stop
My yes to you, withhold

So, goodbye my friend
I have enough
No lack in sight
No need for lust

Dear You,

*How much poison is good for you?
Ask yourself this the next time you
agree with something you know to
be a lie. You exchange your
integrity for temporary satisfaction
or ease because you don't know
who you are. Sis/Bro, living a life
susceptible to intoxication is
unbecoming to who you are. No
one is worth you. God was careful
with you. You should be too.*

*Love,
Tiana*

impaired

Of all the drugs I've taken,
Your lies were my favorite

They consoled me
And told me I was free

They dried my tears
Though they caused the fear

They soothed my mind
Though they created the bind

I thought they were my friends
Because they cared about my lens

They painted pretty pictures for
me
But the paint vanished quickly

They were versatile in nature
A perfect mix on paper

Some I swallowed, some I smoked
But the side effects were cloaked

Blurred vision
Sweaty palms
Short breath
An eerie calm

Is this how free feels?
Lungs full of lies
Choking on the smoke you blew
And drowning in my pride?

Cause I agreed with your deceit
I liked the way it made me feel
The illusion fulfilled a hope I had
To feel something real

Real and free feels different when
you're sober
I wish I knew that sooner
Because now I have to detox
Using God's stain remover

Love, Tiana

As He washes me over
And I feel afresh
I can see and I can breathe
Now that I'm out my flesh

No longer will a lie appease me
And intoxicate my love
Because I'm clean and clear now
And I see that I'm beloved.

Dear You,

I want you to consider that maybe God has strategically placed you in this dark place to reveal your significance. This is not something you find, but something He reveals.

Love,
Tiana

searching

It's dark in here and I'm stuck.
Trying to find something with no
luck.

Not sure what it is or what it's like
But all I know is that I need some
light.

It's been a while since I've seen it
I'm not even sure if it can fit

Is it even something I put on?
Or is it something I innately own?

Can I take it out for rounds?
Or match it up pound for pound?

Is it worthy of my finding?
Or is the value now declining?

What exactly am I looking for?
A mask? A match? A door?

The longer I look the more I don't
know
The more time I spend the less I
have to show

People drop in to help
Because they see me by myself

But I don't know what to say
So I keep looking desperately until
they go away

I think I'm getting closer
Because this feeling's getting
bolder

My heart rate is rising like I know
it's near
I only wish I knew what I was
looking for or why I'm even here

I peer behind furniture, under rugs,
and tables too
Behind the curtains and under the
rack of shoes

Maybe it's not even in here,
Feels like I've been looking for
years

And the more I look the less I find
This must be what it feels like to
be blind

I finally give up, there's no use I
think
To find that missing thing

I sit on the floor
And a sweet small whisper says
what are you looking for?

I respond "I don't know but I'm
tired of looking here"
He says that's okay, just be of
good cheer

I have something to show you
It's here, take a look
Before me was a mirror
Then my whole body shook

It was me I was the thing
That I was looking for
But it took a holy silence
For me to hear the Lord

He told me I was perfect
But there's nothing I could do
But sit here and be quiet
While He revealed to me the Truth

The truth is that I was free
But held captive in my mind
So I searched for my significance
But that was a waste of time

Truth is that in my darkest hour
I thought I couldn't see
But The light I needed in this
space
Was deep inside of me

He pierced the veil When I stopped
looking
And uncovered His light in me
Then I began to see the Truth
That He was the Master key

Silence with Him revealed a peek
Into His master plan
To bring me back to oneness with
Him
And into His careful hands.

healing.

Dear You,

Giving up your past life can be unsettling. Sometimes we don't have the language for what we want or why we feel so disconnected from our new path. Sis/Bro, there's grace and so much love for you in that space. Don't be afraid to acknowledge your cravings and submit them to God.

Love,
Tiana

cravings

Getting saved ..
Saying yes to God..
To be like them.

I want to fit and
I want it to make sense.
I want to have the You came, I saw,
then I went comment.

Instead, I'm questioning the curves
I have left from the last purge I
had when I was broken. Shattered
even. Leaving tiny pieces of grief
of what I used to be.

Agreeable.
Afraid to say what I think 'cause
what think might come off as a
mink mink to your soul.

Avoidant.
I don't fight.
I don't argue.

I just sit quietly here 'cause I'd rather be over there. I don't care.

Amiable
'cause if I'm not, you might talk about me and make me cry. I won't die but it would feel like it inside. I've prided myself on knowing what's right and doing it but now it's like what's right was wrong but I wanted it.

To be right that is...
To not fight that is...
To be liked that is....

What I wanted, I got for years on end until I was shattered. Unable to be pieced together. An image of imperfection doused in deep conviction.

Dangerous.

Insatiable cravings

To be holy and whole.
To have my 80 and my 20
To be straight and upright
To not look down when I'm afraid
To move relentlessly forward
To take everyone who came with
me
To hold in what I need to pour out
To love and not be broken
Dangerous.
The things I tasted and now crave
are the things I can't have because
I'm saved

'Cause
To love is to be broken
To hold in is the prevent the pour
Separations are required
Pit stops are promises too
Looking down is a chance to be
lifted up
Prostrate is the only upright
posture
Sometimes giving 20 gets you 80
Holy and whole are myths

out of the context of the hard
tests of faith.

Are you willing to starve?
Change crave to carve
Let God poke and prod
your soul until it unfolds
That you craved to be saved
Making space for His grace.
Insatiable Cravings.

Love, Tiana

Dear You,

Don't waste anyone's time when you know you lack capacity to hold them. Be honest with yourself and anyone that you're entertaining. If you find it hard to do so, maybe you're not ready and that's okay. Heal first. Pursue later.

Love,
Tiana

47

heal, bae.

It's always "what you doing?"
It's never "hey can I waste your
time for a bit.
You look kinda fine
And like the kind that'll fall for that
line
So I gotta make you mine."

If only you were as real as your
intent
You'd save the words that you
spent and
Write a check to the bank that lent
you that audacity to hide and lie
through the characters you type.

Boy, bye.

What you doing?
Besides wasting your unlimited
texts to test me and stress me
about my dealings and doings

tryna prove your moves towards
me.

Baby, I'm a G.

And in your dreams is the only
place where my attention is
streamed towards you.

I'm not stuck up
I'm just no fool to the cool nice
likes of you, boo.

Ya know, I liked you more before
You got rich from clicks on your
profile pics.

You became filtered and littered
with the filth heard from anxious
men with backs bent and lacked
sense.

Yea, I liked you more before
When I watched you fidget asking
for my digits. It was something

different, something timid, but now
something's missing

Maybe it's integrity embedded in
your pedigree triumphing over the
lies that are witnessed by your
eyes in this time.

Perhaps it's stability and
tranquility you expect from others'
ability to train and sustain you
while you deal with your past pain.

Maybe it's the strength in your
self-think to make you move past
the brink of breaking every
generational link
Perhaps your strength is
paradoxically weakened by the soil
that you steep in. Enraptured by
the weekend and the depends of
your freak ends.

You're better than that baby, but I
can't spare the change to arrange
for your change to take place.

So take the time that you're taking
to prove your take is worth staking
my truth and pour into your soul
releasing control to heal.

So what you doing?

I hope you're getting better babe,
being honest by the letter.

Adding pressure to the investors
to pay back that audacity that
undermines the integrity and
transparency that's yours and mine
when you hit my line to invest your
time into mine.

Dear You,

Allow relational disappointment to serve as a trigger for evaluation. Ask questions, reflect on what you've received, and what you've given. Be sober in this evaluation because our hearts are biased, especially when they're broken. You'll be tempted to place blame instead of extending grace. Sis/Bro, it is possible that you're not as blameless or selfless as your heart wants you to believe.

Love,
Tiana

selfish

I started a breakup letter
I got to four words this time
"<u>What's</u> <u>wrong</u> <u>with</u> <u>you</u>"
I know that's the nicest thing to
ask
But I don't understand.

You take my hand and say you
want more
Then lead me through your heart's
exit door

I didn't ask for this if I'm honest
I was chilling on the cool side of
your pillow

But you decided to flip me over
shine light on my love only to
deny me access to yours

What is wrong with you?
No, seriously.
Let me help you.

Love, Tiana

I'm trying to understand the
workings of your mind and why
you think it's fine to pick me up
and lay me to the side.

Or perhaps it just happened
an anomaly if you will.

Perhaps you held me
And I got too heavy

Maybe you were strong enough to
lift me up but not to put me down.

You dropped me. Carelessly. And
somehow I'm apologetic because I
know you had a good reason. Well,
I hope you did. Did you?

Wait, did I?
Know that you'd drop me, that is?
Were there signs I overlooked for
the sake of being had?
Now parts of me are dislocated
due to your, I mean my
carelessness.

Because I saw the way your hands
quivered when I said I love you. It
was as if the uncertainty in you
could feel the uncertainty in me.

I wanted to be wanted
You wanted to be needed
You fulfilled my want when you
held me
And I fulfilled yours when I let you

As long as the wants were active
we were good, but something
changed.
It's like you care more about the
hands you hold me with more than
you care about me.

Now you don't care to be needed,
you just want to be and I don't
blame you. Because I want that
too. To be, that is. Free from an
expired expectation.

Perhaps the reason you dropped
me was the same reason why I let
you hold me?

Because you wanted to,
I mean I wanted you to.

Two hearts.
Guarded, I mean chained.
To themselves.
Serving themselves.
Sacrificing themselves.
Selfishly.

Maybe our needs became clearer
when our wants were being met
and we still felt empty.
And when the scales hit the
ground so did I.

Collateral damage.

But I never considered the aches
your hands felt holding on to
someone so fragile.

Someone whose whole world
depended on you.
Someone who needed constant
attention, assurance, and
assistance.

That is heavy.

I'm not saying I'm not worth it, but
I'm acknowledging the weight I
was too careless, I mean selfish to
notice.

Maybe I served my purpose, and
you served yours, selflessly. Now
it's time that we move forward
selfishly.

Dear You,

I've had people expect me to place them at the center of my world. This manifested as awe whenever I revealed my truth unapologetically on a first date. They thought that they had a hand in providing a safe space for me, but I found safety long before them. It was nothing special about them that provoked the revelation of the real me. I had learned that showing up as anyone other than me was deception and the manifestation of bondage. I was finally free. Sis/Bro, I pray that same freedom is revealed to you because they're not that special, but you are.

Love,
Tiana

you're not that special

My care with you is not subject to
or dependent on you

Yes I'm open, but that's because
I'm tired of being closed.

Yes I'm gentle, but that's because
I'm tired of being hard.

Yes I'm patient, but I'm tired of
rushing out of time

My exhaustion of the things of old
just happens to benefit you.

And I love this for you.
Because you get the "tired yet
free" version of me
But don't think that you're the
reason.

If you do, then when I evolve again
you'll think it's because of you
when it's actually because of me.

You see, I was once a victim of
someone else's expectations
Pushed around by their
uncertainty
Held back by their fears
Pulled down by their past,
But I got tired
And found rest in the present.

So when I'm here, I fully hear
And when I feel, it extends to the
field of my zeal
So when I laugh it's from my soul
When I speak, you can bet it's in
prose

When I listen, it's intently
When I see, it's soberly

I'm here.
Not waiting to be somewhere

Love, Tiana

I know it's rare,
But absent from peril.
It's just who I am
You're not that special.

Dear You,

Loving the idea of someone is
often how we stay longer, tolerate
more, and sometimes settle for
less. Sis/Bro, don't be so caught up
on the idea of person that you
disregard their reality.

Love,
Tiana

be who you were

Be the person who sat and
listened for hours as I rambled
about life's complications, plans,
and goals

Be the person who had time to
explore my curves and the
changes I had undergone from
life's last lesson

Be the person who gave me grace
when I stumbled and held me up
when I fainted.

Be the person who chose to stay
when everybody left

Be the person who was honest to
a fault and who opened up to me
in spite of your fears

Where's that person?

Maybe you've outgrown me
Maybe I've outgrown you
Maybe my expectations are for an
expired being

Or perhaps that person never
existed
Maybe that was who I thought
you'd be.
Now, who am I to demand you be
someone you never were?

I made it up.
I made you up.

You sat and listened because you
wanted something from me.

The exploration was a means to an
end

Grace is easy to give when you
share stumbling blocks

You stayed because you had
nowhere else to go

Love, Tiana

You were open and honest
because discretion was never a
topic you mastered.

Man, I thought you were mine,
To have and hold
But that's what I made you
You never agreed to the terms of
my imagination.

Dear You,

You're no one's martyr. Their life and love are valuable, but not at the expense of yours.

Love,
Tiana

careful with you

Make no sudden movements,
fix your face just right,
don't blink too fast or
you might start a fight

Don't nod too much,
don't talk too hard,
just gaze intently
until this moment parts

Apologize swiftly.
Yes, even if you're right.
It's not hard to be wrong
at the expense of a good night

I know this is a lot
but this is just the norm
of how I think about you when
you're in rare form

My thoughts begin to jumble,
and my heart begins to race.

Love, Tiana

I've never been good with back
and forth so here's to your first
place.

I love you. This you know is true
but how I can be free?
Free from the damaged you and
free from the careful me.

But is that even love at all?
To be free from all the care?
Or is that just a cop out from the
duty to love we share?

It feels like all the weight's on me
to keep this thing alive. I don't
know how much more I have to
give before I lose my stride.

I feel like I'm engulfed with you
and all that you require
maybe it's time to let you go and
let our love expire.

Love, Tiana

But what would you do if I let go
would you sink or would you
swim?
would you blame me if you fell
and say I left you on a limb?

I'm scared to leave you by yourself
but my help to you has damaged
me.
Maybe it's time to exchange
goodbyes
so I can handle me carefully.

Dear You,

You're not the mother to motherless, or father to the fatherless. You are not responsible for the total satisfaction of another grown person. It's draining when you take on a responsibility that was never yours. Pray for them. Relieve yourself of the unnecessary weight of someone else's happiness, security, and self-esteem.

Love,
Tiana

you're not my responsibility

Your looks and likes
Your barks and bites
Your past and pardons
Your bags and bargains
They're not my responsibility.

I am not responsible for
Making sure your honor and ego
are intact
Assuring you of your worth
Reinforcing the comfort zones of
your past

I am not responsible for making
sure you notice me
Curating a look you can't ignore
Echoing the sound of your favorite
influencer
Providing a reality you're not ready
for.

I am not responsible for you.

Nor am I responsible for me.
I thought I was until I was left
empty
Gassing you up with the fumes of
my insecurity

I thought I was until responsibility
wrapped around my neck like a
noose or necklace laced with
accountability

You came at a cost that I could've
afforded had I not already been
purchased.

I was bought with a life
And somehow I lost my way
I laid my worth aside
And picked up your tab to pay

I'm sorry I can't afford you..
Because I couldn't afford me.
At no fault to you of course
You're just not my responsibility.

Love, Tiana

Maybe you, too, should dial it back
Remember from whence you came
Take note of Whose you really are
And I will do the same.

Dear You,

It's okay to reserve yourself. No one is entitled to you or a specific version of you. Many of us are spreading ourselves thin trying to keep up with the expectations of those we love or those we want to love us. We adopt conformation because we don't believe that God has made a space for us in someone else's life. Sis/Bro, you're already loved by the Most High God. You were carefully curated by His hands. So, your status moving forward is reserved.

Love,
Tiana

reserved

Too much access lowers value
This I know to be true
I say this in hopes you'll take it
And be more choosey with you

What you don't understand
You'll never esteem
So get to know you
Before you share you with me

Know that you're worthy of a wait
No need to rush to be served
Take you time and take theirs
That's the least that you deserve

Stop making up the difference
And let them come to you
You're not some beggar on the
street
You're the Cinderella shoe

Not made to fit just anybody
You're dainty and precise
So, stop acting like you're a
commonplace
And letting others roll your life's
dice

Set your standard
And stick to it
Be okay with leaving
While they're bidding

Because you're not just an option
You're more than they deserve
So, no they can't sit with you while
you wait
Because your access is reserved.

Dear You,

It's okay to want and position
yourself to encounter easy things.
The key is to acknowledge your
desire for ease and have courage
to pursue it.

Love,
Tiana

benches to tables

Benches come with no obligation
to commune.
They don't expect an exchange.
They offer a sense of settling for
all who partake.
They don't assume consumption or
assure production.
They provide opportunities to
share a perspective with another.
The only participation required is
choosing to sit; not to be served
or serve, but to be.

Benches are easy for me.
They're not the hard things that
coincide with my will to fight,
discuss, negotiate, fix, or serve.
They let me be and see and
choose to share.

Now, tables require a bit more
from me that I'm not always willing
to give. It's rude to be silent. It's

frowned upon if you don't
contribute to the spread. The view
is limited to what's on the table or
who's seated around the table.
And honestly, I'd rather know what
you see when you're sitting next to
me.

How does this view look to you?
What colors do you see?
What stands out to you the most?
and if that's too much,
silence is acceptable.
Sharing space is enough.

So, what do I bring to the table?
Well, nothing.
But the nothing I bring to a table
is everything that a bench requires
of me.

Love, Tiana

Dear You,

Sometimes we know what we want,
we know how to get what we want,
but we lack the knowledge to
handle what we want. An
independent woman can be a
challenge for power hungry,
insecure, weak men. Her
independence should not
intimidate you. If it does, be honest
with yourself about it. Right after
that, find a way to make her life
easier. I can almost guarantee that
she is doing what she HAS to do
and she wouldn't mind ease being
added to her life.

Love,
Tiana

wait

To the man pursuing that single
independent woman, be patient.

You may like that she stands on
her own. You may love how she
gets things done, but this may
cause her to be less dependent on
your opinion and her opinion less
appealing to your tenure.

You're a man.
And she's strong.

Not like but similar to the likes of
you. Impetuous. Which serves as
an impediment and detriment of
your ego if you let it.

She goes left when you say right
and she stays put when you say fly

She's less likely to move when you
say 'cause when she's moves she

don't play and the last stray lead
her astray so she'll stay. Until she's
safe.

Understand that those traits are
necessary for the everyday life she
lives. Also, understand that those
traits won't change overnight just
because you desire she be softer.

Some of us want to be soft but
soft doesn't cut it when decisions
have to be made and bills have to
be paid.

Personally, I haven't mastered the
switch. My eyes twitch when
there's glitch in consistency. It
reminds me of sixteen being waist
deep in empty expectancy.

So I'll go before there's hope and
if there's hope then I'll slope into
the depths of nope.
'Cause nah, I'm good.

So you see, we're not the softest
ladies in the bunch but we're the
ones that come through in a
crunch.

I promise the same things you
don't like are the same reasons
you vibe with us so be patient.

Be patient and wait for the
ablation of red tape that protects
us from us.

Be kind to us and you'll find that
the fine wine you waited so
patiently for has settled into the
new skin you poured her in when
you waited.

Love, Tiana

healed.

Dear You,

The idea that although someone
has options and chooses you is
satisfying. Add to that, this person
respects your boundaries and
aligns with the goal to grow, hm,
chef's kiss. When these ideas
become reality, you become
protective, which sometimes leads
to a spiral of negative thinking.
Sis/Bro, be present. The idea is real
for now. The past nor the future
matters. For now, there's now.

Love,
Tiana

freelance

hm, urges that I have for this man
purges me into this discouraging
world.

Hence, making way for confusion
and exclusion of emotions.
Broadening these horizons with
austere precautions.

Consistency matched and attached
with persistency fighting on this
battlefield of land mines. Lord, I'm
Praying not to lose this time.

Setting standards then breaking
boundaries is such a casualty, but
we fight through the physicalities
and principalities to get it right

'Cause this ain't that roses are red,
violets are blue type thing, nor is it
that 3 months on and 3 months

off type fling. This that make it last
forever type scene.

The future being completely in
reach, understanding that God's
only preparing us for destiny.

So, the past we had in comparison
to the revelation we have has no
place in this space of grace

Having a man with somewhere to
go and something to do is rare,
but having to had shared this man
is one thing that's not fair, and I
can't bare the thought.

The thought of the past and
impact SHE had.
His hugs, she had
His lips, she had
His body, she had
His mind, she had.

She being all of the females that
partook in experiences HAD,

87

but like I said that's the past. It's not about the other and another because drake said we're perfect for each other because it's not about what SHE HAD it's about what I HAVE and that's a chance to clear a path and do the math of his heart.

Adding the positive, subtracting the negative, doing what's imperative of his woman. That's me, I HAVE that title, that responsibility, that role, that chance to have this freelance man.

Dear You,

*Treat getting to know someone
new as if you are doing a survey
on a piece of real estate. Study
them. Don't assume. Just observe.
Gather data to paint a clear picture
of who they are and what they
have and whether it matches what
you want.*

*Love,
Tiana*

survey

I want to see everything you own
Nothing physical of course
But fruit from the seeds you've
sown

I want to know your whys
I want to know your how's
How much land does peace take
now

Help me trace how your woulds
and coulds
Switched to doings and dids
I wanna know you

Let me see the scars you barred
yourself from seeing. And your
heart's bruises from the last
beating.

Don't be afraid.
I won't hurt you.
I know those words echo the last
wrong turn you took but it's true.

Love, Tiana

Just let me see you.
From your calloused hands
To your wrinkles and grays
I want to survey your land

Show me everything
Inside and out
Not to judge you
Just to know what you're about

What do you like?
Where is your treasure?
How is your soul?
What is your pleasure?

I'd love to know more
If you have the time
to share yourself with me
To see if you're mine.

Dear You,

Love laced together by our Creator is beautiful. It's humble. It's not proud or loud. It's safe. If you do not find these traits within a connection, it is not love.

Love,
Tiana

love

It's patient and kind and all the
things that align with you, love

Not that you are greater than or
equal to the One we know to be
true.

But to acknowledge the truth:
I've never seen the proof of
something so pure and unsure of
its worth.

I mean its girth could encapsulate
the Earth.
When it shines, It then hides.
It's forced out then collides with
me.

Love, I know it's not easy
Being big but feeling small
Stooping down whilst standing tall
But that's love.

Love, Tiana

My love is subtle.
It's mild and meek
And it peaks at the feat
Of my heart in your hands
I'm stranded.

Your love and mine have banded
At the seams and it seems
To cover Insecurity and Inability
Making way for stability
By way of the Trinity we call Love.

94

Dear You,

*We know that love is patient, but
we're not always patient with love.
Sis/Bro, take your time with love.
It's not something to be rushed into
or through. When offense comes
contend for it. When love is
threatened, defend it. Choose it,
every time in everything.*

Love,
Tiana

patient with love

It's the exchange between silence
and offense that offends our
nature to defend ourselves.

It's the "I'm hurt but I'll do" and
"I'll risk playing the fool for you,"
love.

It's the "I" wants and "I" needs
being brought to their knees to
appease "their" wants and "their"
needs.

It's the cleaning of messes with
tears through fears, stressors, and
pressure; love.

It's not all bad but when the light
is snuffed out and the will is cuffed
down, will you crush the doubt
that surrounds the sound of love?
Will you contend for the mending
of every broken piece and part,

Love, Tiana

while searching in the dark for
peace and belief in love?

Will you try to fill the silence
With meaningless explanations
To defend pride and ego?

Or will you sit in the silence
together, unyielding, fully
persuaded that love will win?

When love leaves, will you call for
it?

Patience from love and patience
for love are two sides of the same
coin. The journey of love requiring
both.

So are you ready
To travail from and for love.

Dear You,

Many of us would love to hurry and skip to the end of our love stories. Sis/Bro, I encourage you to sip your love like a fine glass of wine. Allow it to sober you with every sip. The time will come when the fields of your love are white and ready to be harvested. Until then, you can wait.

Love,
Tiana

The One

I can't wait to be the one to
experience every moon and sun
with you.

I can't wait to be the one who
rides the tidal waves of life with
you.

I can't wait to be the one who
shares the weight of pain and
purpose with you.

Knowing I can't fix it but maybe
when it's all twisted I can hold you
together while the Father mends
it.

I don't want to be the one you run
from, but the one you run with out
of every pit you happen to land in.

Saying I can't wait is an
understatement.

This passion is burning like hot
pavement
And the basement of my heart
can't take this
I'm breaking

But I'm patient.
Patiently waiting.
Like a patient in waiting.

"Doctor, Is it time now?"
I'm feeling out of time now.

But what's time to every Sun?
Just a temporal sign to The One.

So, I can wait.

For every moon and every sun,
Every trial and every run,
Every wave against the shore,
Every pain from every pour.

I can wait.

Love, Tiana

For every pit and every fall,
Every purpose and every call,
Every person you're to be,
Every chance I get see.

I can wait.

For every rising and every setting,
Every striving and every getting,
Every line of time undone,
Every moment to be the one.

Dear You,

Privacy is the best relationship hack. If you can keep your relationship private, do it. Don't be jealous of the couples who publicize their relationships on social media. It's okay to cultivate a private, safe space for the relationship you're building.

Love,
Tiana

formed

We were
Shaped in a dark room
Under the black Light
Exposing every speck and
Hidden from sight

We were

Run through water
From dirty to clean
Ridding every blemish
From crowds unseen

We were

Ground under pressure
Spit out piece by piece
Thrown back into the darkness
To resolve in peace

We were

Built in private
In ways no man can teach
Unprecedented growth
That no man can leech

Now
We're steady.
Unwavering in love
Our portion is safety
And the fullness thereof.

Dear You,

Allow your love to be as a compilation of beautiful photographs. Take note of how light and darkness interact because it wouldn't be love if you didn't have both.

Love,
Tiana

photo

It's not just your smile
Although it curves just right
Teeth straight and white
Shining light around you.

It's not just your lips
Although they're soft and ripe
Not parting for strife but
Speaking nothing but life

It's not just your eyes
Although they're dark and deep
And lonely yet meek
Sneaking peeks into me

Although these are parts and
pieces
They'll never be the whole nor
reasons for my need to see.
I don't want the smile without the
lips
Like you don't want my thighs
without the hips

I need your eyes to testify that
what lies inside aligns with my
sign of life.

The pieces of you have to match
the pieces within me as broken as
they are they're something I need
to see.

Do my eyes match the depth of
yours?
Do my lips pour the same as
yours?
Do my teeth align just like your
kind?
I wouldn't erase anything on your
face
'cause it mirrors what I see from
day to day

The depth the curve the light in
our space
Shows the picture of our beauty
when we're face to face.

Dear You,

Perhaps the love that we're familiar with requires more than we thought. Perhaps the television shows and movies made it look easier than it is. Sis/Bro, sit with God and lay before Him your understanding of love. Ask Him to reveal Himself in your pieces. Who better to teach you about love than the One who is one with love?

Love,
Tiana

what if love

Was shown through the endurance
of suffering?
What if the presence of pain
proves that love is also present?

Perhaps love isn't the absence of
hard things but the embodiment
of all things
All being the good and the bad,
the happy and the sad,
the healing and the pain, the loss
and the gain

What if God's love wasn't getting
all we deserve but by His mercy
not getting all we desire.

It's His love that keeps things
together and that same love that
breaks things apart to be brought
into His wholeness.

So love, God's love, is made up of peeks into your destiny. He considered your definition of love and decided that it wasn't good enough. So, He's orchestrated your high and lows and surplus and deficits to align with His abundance.

It's not your love that will mend the bond and destroy the enmity between fathers and sons and mothers and daughters. It's a revelation of His love.

It's the revelation that love actually covers a multitude of sins. It doesn't extinguish, enable, empathize with or expose sins but it covers them.

It's the revelation that you don't always get to choose, and God has appointed things and people to choose you.

That's family.

The ones who are appointed to
choose you so that God's love can
be made manifest in its rawest
form.

The ones you bear with.
The ones you forgive.
The ones you lend and give to.
The ones you're patient with.
The ones you're kind to.

That's family.
That's love.

Dear You,

Have you ever experienced a holy love? A love so specific that only God could've given it. If you haven't, I encourage you to spend more time with Him because He has given you a blueprint of how love is supposed to look and feel. Sometimes we settle for altered versions of love because we haven't familiarized ourselves with the love from our Father. You should be so familiar with His love that you reject everything that doesn't align with what you know His love to be.

Love,
Tiana

familiar

Your love feels like home.
Cozy.
Like Grandpa's house in winter
Warm.
Never requiring anything but rest
Easy.
But works as the perfect void filler.
Diligent.

It looks for ways to consider
Caring
Takes note of all requests
Attentive
A place where peace resides
Settled
Where patience passes the test
Mature

It feels like family
Secure
Like standing Sunday dinner dates
Consistent
Likes my time in worship

Free
It loses track of time and occupies
the wait
Patient

Oh how sweet it is
to have something to compare it
to
A dream fulfilled
Almost like God knew

He embedded you with His love
And surrounded me with the same
I guess so that I could recognize it
When along in time you came.

Dear You,

There's nothing wrong with having an uneventful relationship. It breeds contentment. Some of us are conditioned to think boring is bad, but it's not. There's nothing like having a love that is stable, predictable, and consistent.

Love,
Tiana

regular love

I want a love that bores a stranger
When I try to explain that our
everyday is every day

That we love each other like
tomorrow is promised

That we hold every moment as
close as the laundry sheets are
folded

That our love encapsulates tears
to water the plants in our garden.
It flows together like the color
palette in the living room.

It's soft like the fluffy pillows on
our bed.

It's seasoned as well as Sunday's
pot roast.

The love that takes time to
marinate and takes even longer to
cook.
It takes time to cool before you
consume it.
And even then you have to take
small bites and chew thoroughly.

A love that requires patience
That chooses to wait.
That doesn't hasten to anger but
calms to the tune of the tea
kettles ring for the afternoon tea.

Uncomplicated

Void of glitz and glitter yet full of
color
Not extraordinary like mauve and
periwinkle
But basic, primary, foundational

The love that is the root of our
family tree
Deeply hidden beneath the ground
Inconceivable yet essential

Roots that aren't loud
They don't tell you what they're
doing
They keep no record of everything
done
They just do everyday, every day.

Regular love.

connect with the author

If this book has inspired, encouraged, or helped you in any way, leave a review on the platform from which you purchased it. Then, visit www.pstianamarie.com or email pstianamarie@gmail.com with any feedback you'd like to provide and to receive updates on new projects from the author. Follow Tiana Marie on Instagram at pstianamarie and add her on Facebook.

www.ingramcontent.com/pod-product-compliance
Lightning Source LLC
Chambersburg PA
CBHW071030280326
41935CB00011B/1524